Puma Punku And Ti Strangest Ancient Site On Earth?

Brien Foerster

Quadcopter view of Puma Punku

Pumapunku or Puma Punku (Aymara and Quechua puma cougar, puma, punku door, Hispanicized Puma Puncu) is part of a large temple complex or monument group that is part of the Tiwanaku Site near Tiwanaku, in western Bolivia. It is believed to date to AD 536 and later.

Tiwanaku is significant in Inca traditions because it is believed to be the site where the world was created. In Aymara, Puma Punku's name means "The Door of the Puma". Puma Punku complex consists of an unwalled western court, a central unwalled esplanade, a terraced platform mound that is faced with stone, and a walled eastern court.

Quadcopter view of Puma Punku with massive slabs shown.

Puma Punku is a terraced earthen mound that is faced with blocks. It is 167.36 meters (549.1 feet) wide along its north–south axis and 116.7 meters (383 feet) long along its east–west axis. On the northeast and southeast corners of Puma Punku, it has 20 meter (66-foot) wide projections that extend 27.6 meters (91 feet) north and south from the rectangular mound.

The eastern edge of Puma Punku is occupied by what is called the Plataforma Litica.. This structure consists of a stone terrace that is 6.75 by 38.72 meters (22.1 by 127.0 feet) in dimension. This terrace is paved with multiple enormous stone blocks. It contains the largest stone slab found in both Puma Punku and Tiwanaku Site, measuring 7.81 meters (25.6 feet) long, 5.17 meters

(17.0 feet) wide and averages 1.07 meters (3 feet 6 inches) thick. Based upon the specific gravity of the red sandstone from which it was carved, this stone slab has been estimated to weigh 131 metric tons.

View of part of the Platforma litica

The other stonework and facing of Puma Punku consists of a mixture of andesite and red sandstone. Puma Punku's core consists of clay, while the fill underlying selected parts of its edge consists of river sand and cobbles instead of clay. Excavations have supposedly documented "three major building epochs, in addition to small repairs and remodeling".

At its peak, Puma Punku is thought to have been "unimaginably wondrous," adorned with polished metal plaques, brightly colored ceramic and fabric ornamentation, and visited by costumed citizens, elaborately dressed priests, and elites decked in exotic jewelry. Current understanding of this complex is limited due to its age, the lack of a written record, and the current deteriorated state of the structures due to treasure hunting, looting, stone mining for building stone and railroad ballast, and natural weathering.

Slightly closer view

View of partial excavation at Puma Punku

The area within the kilometer separating Puma Punku and Kalasasaya complexes has been surveyed using ground-penetrating radar, magnetometry, induced electrical conductivity, and magnetic susceptibility. The geophysical data collected from these surveys and excavations have revealed the presence of numerous man-made structures in the area between the Puma Punku and Kalasasaya complexes. These structures include the wall foundations of buildings and compounds, water conduits, pool-like features, revetments, terraces, residential compounds, and widespread gravel pavements, all of which now lie buried and hidden beneath the modern ground's surface.

Massive red sandstone slabs

Researchers have worked to determine the age of the Puma Punku complex since the discovery of the

Tiwanaku site. As noted by Andean specialist, W. H. Isbell, professor at Binghamton University, a radiocarbon date was obtained by Vranich from organic material from the lowermost and oldest layer of mound-fill forming Puma Punku. This layer was deposited during the first of three proposed construction epochs and dates the initial construction of Puma Punku to supposedly 536 to 600 AD. (1510 ±25 B.P. C14, calibrated date). Since the radiocarbon date came from the lowermost and oldest layer of mound-fill underlying the andesite and sandstone stonework, the stonework must have been constructed sometime after 536 to 600 AD. The excavation trenches of Vranich show that the clay, sand, and gravel fill of the Pumapunku complex lie directly on the sterile middle Pleistocene sediments. These excavation trenches also demonstrated the lack of any pre-Andean Middle Horizon cultural deposits within the area of the Tiwanaku Site adjacent to the Puma Punku complex.

As stated earlier the largest of these stone blocks is 7.81 meters long, 5.17 meters wide, averages 1.07 meters thick, and is estimated to weigh about 131 metric tons. The second largest stone block found within Puma Punku is 7.90 meters (25.9 feet) long, 2.50 meters (8 feet 2 inches) wide, and averages 1.86 meters (6 feet 1 inch) thick. Its weight has been estimated to be 85.21 metric tons. Both of these stone blocks are part of the Plataforma Litica and composed of red sandstone. Based upon detailed petrographic and chemical analyses of samples from both individual stones and known quarry sites, archaeologists concluded that these and other red sandstone blocks were transported up a steep incline from a quarry near Lake Titicaca roughly 10 kilometers (6.2 miles) away. Smaller andesite blocks that were used for stone facing and carvings came from quarries within the Copacabana Peninsula about 90 kilometers (56 miles) away from and across Lake Titicaca from Puma Punku and the rest of the Tiwanaku Site.

Large andesite slab and 4 H blocks

Archaeologists argue that the transport of these stones was accomplished by the large labor force of ancient Tiwanaku. Several theories have been proposed as to how this labor force transported the stones, although these theories remain speculative. Two of the more common proposals involve the use of llama skin ropes and the use of ramps and inclined planes.

End view of the Platforma litica

In assembling the walls of Puma Punku, each stone was finely cut to interlock with the surrounding stones. The blocks were fit together like a puzzle, forming load-bearing joints without the use of mortar. One common engineering technique involves cutting the top of the lower stone at a certain angle, and placing another stone on top of it which was cut at the same angle. The precision with which these angles have been used to create flush joints is indicative of a highly sophisticated knowledge of stone-cutting and a thorough understanding of descriptive geometry. Many of the joints are so precise that not even a razor blade will fit between the stones. Much of the masonry is

8

characterized by accurately cut rectilinear blocks of such uniformity that they could be interchanged for one another while maintaining a level surface and even joints. However, the blocks do not have the same dimensions, although they are close. The blocks were so precisely cut as to suggest the possibility of prefabrication and mass production, technologies far in advance of the Tiwanaku's Inca successors hundreds of years later. Some of the stones are in an unfinished state, showing some of the techniques used to shape them. They were initially pounded by stone hammers, which can still be found in numbers on local andesite quarries, creating depressions, and then slowly ground and polished with flat stones and sand. At least that is the official academics' theory, though they have likely not interviewed stone masons or engineers to see if any of this was feasible for the bronze age Tiwanaku people. Tiwanaku engineers were also supposedly adept at developing a civic infrastructure at this complex, constructing functional irrigation systems, hydraulic mechanisms, and waterproof sewage lines.

Puma Punku was a large earthen platform mound with three levels of stone retaining walls. Its layout is thought to have resembled a square. To sustain the weight of these massive structures, Tiwanaku architects were supposedly meticulous in creating foundations, often fitting stones directly to bedrock or digging precise trenches and carefully filling them with layered sedimentary stones to support large stone blocks.

Another view of the Platforma litica

Modern day engineers argue that the base of the Pumapunku temple was constructed using a technique called layering and depositing. By alternating layers of sand from the interior and layers of composite from the exterior, the fills would overlap each other at the joints, essentially grading the contact points to create a sturdy base.

Notable features at Puma Punku are I-shaped architectural clamps, which are composed of a unique copper-arsenic-nickel bronze alloy. These I-shaped clamps were also used on a section of canal found at the base of the Akapana pyramid at Tiwanaku. The clamps were used to hold the blocks comprising the walls and bottom of stone-lined canals that drain sunken courts. I-clamps of unknown composition were used to hold together the massive slabs that formed Puma Punku's four large platforms.

Examples of the I-shaped clamp insert areas

In the south canal of Puma Punku, the I-shaped cramps were cast in place. In sharp contrast, the clamps used at the Akapana canal were fashioned by the cold hammering of copper-arsenic-nickel bronze ingots. This by itself suggests two separate cultures were present and likely at different times because smelting bronze at an altitude of 13,000 feet would be extremely complex and difficult. The unique copper-arsenic-nickel bronze alloy is also found in metal artifacts within the region between Tiwanaku and San Pedro de Atacama during the late Middle Horizon around 600–900, but this does not prove when they were originally made.

More I-shaped clamp insert areas in andesite

It is theorized by some academics that the Puma Punku complex as well as its surrounding temples, the Akapana pyramid, Kalasasaya, Putuni, and Kerikala functioned as spiritual and ritual centers for the Tiwanaku. This area might have been viewed as the center of the Andean world, attracting pilgrims from far away to marvel in its beauty. These structures transformed the local landscape; Puma Punku was purposely integrated with Illimani mountain, a sacred peak that the Tiwanaku possibly believed to be home to the spirits of their dead.

This realm was believed to have existed between heaven and Earth.

Red sandstone block with depressions

The Tiwanaku civilization and the use of these temples appears to some to have peaked from 700 to 1000 AD, by which point the temples and surrounding area may have been home to some 400,000 people. An extensive infrastructure had been developed, including a complex irrigation system that extended more than 30 square miles (80 km2) to support cultivation of potatoes, quinoa, corn and other various crops. At its peak the Tiwanaku culture dominated the entire Lake Titicaca basin as well as portions of Bolivia and Chile.

Interesting andesite stone with many drill holes

This culture seems to have dissolved rather abruptly sometime around 1000 AD, and researchers are still seeking answers as to why. A likely scenario involves rapid environmental change, possibly involving an extended drought. Unable to produce the massive crop yields necessary for their large population, the Tiwanaku are argued to have scattered into the local mountain ranges, only to disappear shortly thereafter. Puma Punku is thought to have been abandoned before it was finished. This is definitely the case as you shall see as we proceed in this book.

The author with the H blocks

As you can already tell, the difference between the text above, taken from standard academic sources and the photos do not match up.

Most of what we know about both Puma Punku comes from the 4 to 5 decades of excavations done by Bolivian archaeologist Arturo Posnansky, who wrote 2 massive volumes in great detail about what he found and his theories as regards how old Tiwanaku and Puma Punku are. His conclusions of the age being more than 10,000 years was laughed at internationally, but as we shall see, the evidence is clear that he was onto something.

Unfinished and finished H blocks

Perhaps the most beguiling of all artifacts at Puma Punku are what are commonly called the H blocks seen above. There are a total of 8 of them in intact condition and 1 broken, and it does not appear that there were ever more of them as some would suggest. Much of the stone removed from Puma Punku and Tiwanaku can be found in the local town of Tiwanaku, having been used in the construction of local buildings, likely beginning when the Spanish first arrived in the 16th century. The stones were moved and used in intact conditions, and those chosen tended to be square or rectangular in shape. The H blocks are odd in design and thus not as suitable for such a recycled use.

Finished on the left and unfinished on the right

What the photo above shows you is that Puma Punku was likely never completed and later we will discuss that it was likely destroyed by an ancient cataclysm long before the existence of the Tiwanaku people. The stone on the left shows crisp and clean angles on the interior depressions in the center of the stone and two false door impressions; one on the top depression and another on the bottom one. The depressions in the stone on the right are rougher, are curved at the corners and are missing the false doors, thus unfinished. This alone tells us that at least two forms of technology were used to shape the surfaces and depressions; first a roughing tool that left a sand blasted like surface, and then a refining tool establishing incredibly flat surfaces.

Depressions are not 90 degree angles

Also, the depressed areas are not exact right angles, but more akin to dovetail shapes, which some researchers believe were made on purpose because another shaped stone was meant to fit and lock into the depression. However, there are no such matching shapes to be found at either Puma Punku or Tiwanaku and it is unlikely they, if they did exist were taken away for use elsewhere. So, the reasoning behind the dovetail shape is presently unknown.

The idea that much of the stone from Puma Punku was taken to La Paz when the Spanish were constructing that city is highly unlikely taking into account the distance involved.

Backs of 2 of the H blocks

Also, it should be noted that the H blocks are not exactly the same dimensions, and thus the idea that they were mass produced and created in a mold must be rejected. As well, the designs on the backs vary, in some cases greatly, so it is obvious that each one was individually crafted, the questions are how and why, yet to be determined.

Theories have been touted that whole walls were made of H blocks, that a rocket launching ramp was made of them, etc. However, there is no evidence to substantiate such claims.

The author pondering the enigma

What is also curious is that the grey andesite stones affect a physical compass while the red sandstone does not. In some cases the compass needle will move as much as 360 degrees when the compass moves within contact distance of the surface, and in the case of the H blocks the unfinished one does not affect the needle and yet the finished ones cause the needle to move by 90 degrees when slowly moved into the upper and lower depressions.

This is something that standard academia has either ignored or are not aware of, likely due to their insistence that the bronze age Tiwanaku people were the original builders.

Block with precise groove and drill holes in center of photo

Most would think that the magnetic anomalies are the result of the stone simply having iron and or magnetite as part of its composition, but the reasoning is far more complex than that, and is the focus of my current investigations at these locations. As the quarry is more than 70 kilometers away it is clear that the original builders chose the stone partially for its magnetic characteristics, at least in part.

This of course brings up the question of how the stone was moved. As the red sandstone quarry is somewhat around 10 kilometers away, up and over at least one mountain range, academics contend that wooden rollers were used, though no native trees grow in this

21

area as it is above the tree line. Also, the grey andesite quarry is on top of a volcano across Lake Titicaca.

Once again the academics have an answer; reed boats. Taking into account that some of the andesite stones weigh as much as 40 tons, a transportation system like that is quite ridiculous.

Various shapes at Puma Punku

There is no art work to be had at either Puma Punku or Tiwanaku on the original surfaces, though the later Tiwanaku people did do surface carving, rather crudely, on such works as the famous Sun Gate.

What we do have are repeating symbols such as the false door designs and crosses seen above, quite simple but eloquently executed.

Andesite with Tiawanaku relief carving

Lack of obvious art work could indicate that the original makers were far more pragmatic in nature than artistic, building Puma Punku and Tiwanaku to function rather that appease or please. Come along the later Tiwanaku people who found beautiful flat surfaces to work on, and so they etched their deities onto blank canvases.

I am still astonished that most if not all academics cannot clearly see that the relief carving is far cruder than the original surfaces. It is the same case in Egypt where at a site called the Serapeum at Saqqara contains more than 20 granite, syenite and diorite boxes weighing 100 tons a piece and have polished and in some cases very flat surfaces. One has child like glyphs scratched into the surface yet scholars insist that the glyphs and boxes are contemporary with each other.

Flat andesite surface

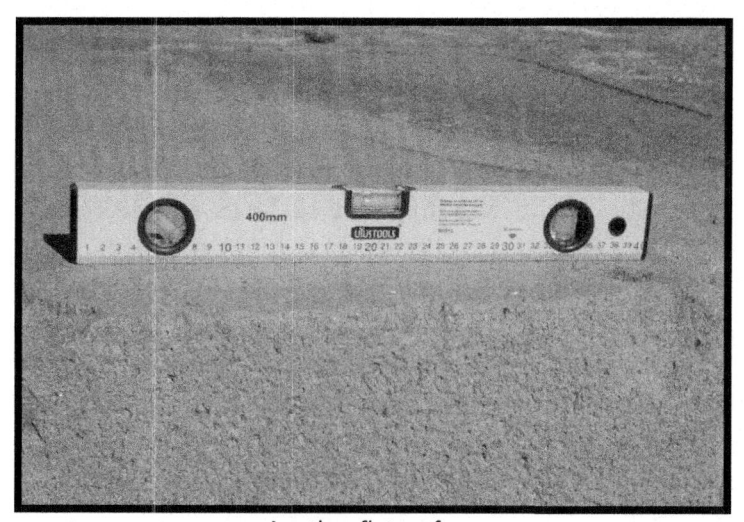

Another flat surface

24

Cross designs

False door fragment

More Puma Punku artifacts

Flat surfaces with strange discoloration

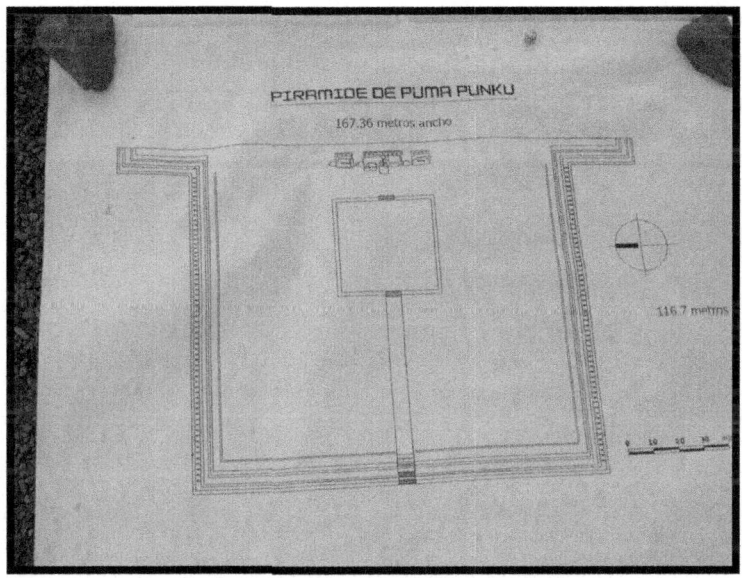

Proposed original Puma Punku design

The above design is how most academics think that Puma Punku looked like when originally discovered. Note the fact that the H blocks and other anomalous shapes are not included. Regarded as simply being a temple constructed by the Tiawanaku people, again they have not taken into account that the Tiawanaku could not have constructed it in the first place, though said Tiwanaku may have used it as a temple of sorts.

The design is quite simple and somewhat graceful in execution, being bilaterally symmetrical with a square depression near the top, which having been excavated can be seen to this day.

It consists of 6 levels, the first 4 being made of tight fitting red sandstone blocks and then the upper 1 of andesite that locks into the sandstone.

The 4 layers of sandstone with andesite missing

This is a major clue as to what the original function of Puma Punku may have been. As the red sandstone is magnetically neutral and the andesite magnetized in some way, shape or form this could infer that the andesite, forming the upper perimeter could have created an energetic field inside the central area of the structure. Not something with a huge amount of energy but perhaps enough to be felt when it was intact
What could such an energy be used for?

4 layers of red sandstone facing Lake Titicaca

Very tightfitting sandstone blocks

Another photo of the perimeter

The unfortunate thing is that reconstruction of the site, as seen on the right side of the above photo was based on speculation and not at all on facts or evidence. Their filling in the upper tiers with clay mud is a presumption, and in fact damages the ability to properly decode Puma Punku.

It is possible that originally there were a second and third series of tiers that also had 4 layers of red sandstone blocks and a 5th of andesite; this could have acted as an energetic/magnetic structure of some form. So was this done to allow the builders to stand in the center and get into alternate states of consciousness in order to access higher functions? A way to broadcast thought energy? Or something as simple or fundamental as a plant enhancing center?

It is well known that magnetism can affect the growth of plants, so it is possible that Puma Punku was built, strange as it may sound as a garden to grow plants whose seeds would become substantially fortified. As life at 13,000 feet above sea level is very harsh with either cloudy conditions or painfully bright sunlight, seed enhancing would be a way to make future plants far more resilient.

Stones projecting out of the wall

It is quite evident that Puma Punku, and to a lesser case Tiwanaku were hit by one or a series of cataclysms in the distant past, and were found by the Tiwanaku people in ruins, partially buried.

Excavated area on the north side

The above photo shows an area that was relatively recently excavated, with more than a meter of clay mud removed, where the people are standing. This shows us that Puma Punku was literally partially buried by a wall of mud that came from Lake Titicaca, likely as the result of the explosion of Cerro Khapia to the north which is a dormant volcano. The eruption would have thrown vast amounts of stone into the lake, and with a corresponding earthquake could have caused a tsunami. The likely timeline of this is about 12,000 years ago as science is being to support as it appears that a global cataclysm happened at that time which affected other ancient places like Egypt, the highlands of Peru, and likely Baalbek in Lebanon and Petra in Jordan.

Partial excavation at Puma Punku

The above photo shows that many broken pieces of Puma Punku were found underground when excavated in the past few years. Such damage would not have been from the Spanish or even Tiwanaku people, but from an enormous force that smashed into Puma Punku and buried parts of it. The unfortunate thing is that archaeologists refuse to digger deeper, as ground penetrating radar has shown that there is at least one large chamber underground at the site, rectangular in shape and clearly artificial.

It is simply an attempt by them to attempt to cover up the true nature of the complexity and antiquity of Puma Punku, because such ideas go against their paradigm.

More evidence of ancient destruction

More destruction

More of Puma Punku in a nearby field

Excavated broken slabs at Tiwanaku

Ancient staircase on the north side of Puma Punku

There are some that believe that Puma Punku was originally a lake port. This is actually supported by some evidence. 12,000 years ago Lake Titicaca was 100 feet higher than it is today, and thus of course was also much larger. The staircase in the above photo appears to be very ancient based on the weathering of the massive slabs of red sandstone that were later repaired with smaller stones by the Tiwanaku culture.

A 110 foot rise in the lake's level, whose shore is presently about 7 miles away would have brought the shoreline basically to where the bottom step is, and supports Arturo Posnansky's claim that Puma Punku and Tiwanaku were first built more than 12,000 years ago.

Antonio Portugal at the staircase

Water channel at Puma Punku

The author in the other water channel

The above 2 photos show the presence of 2 channels at the north end of Puma Punku which are quite perplexing. As they are angled slightly downward from the center out to the ends one could assume they were water channels made to move water from Puma Punku to the surrounding fields and this could in fact be correct, and reinforces the theory that Puma Punku was an agricultural experimental station.

The stones fit together almost perfectly, which is what you would want in a water channel, and bronze clamps, poured into place once held the stones firmly together. The idea that the Tiwanaku people were capable of smelting bronze at an elevation of 13,000 feet above sea level is quite ludicrous, and thus points to a very advanced civilization being present to build Puma Punku.

Horizontal surfaces very level

More complex shapes at Puma Punku

An over 100 ton slab at Puma Punku

Large andesite block in a nearby field

There are also the remains of two large gates at Puma Punku whose original function and placement are unknown. Foolishly the academics actually move them from time to time thus damaging our ability to theoretically reassemble Puma Punku.

One of the Puma Punku gates

They are smaller than the famous Sun Gate at Tiwanaku that as well was likely moved from its original location and the one above has depressions in it but no Tiwanaku culture glyphs. It is then very possible that it was left where the Tiwanaku found it whereas the other one does have glyphs on it and thus likely that the Tiwanaku used it as a ceremonial gate. There is also a fourth gate on top of the Akapana pyramid which we will be discussing shortly that is broken and does not have any glyphs on it.

Gate at Puma Punku with glyphs near the top

Elongated skull found near Puma punku

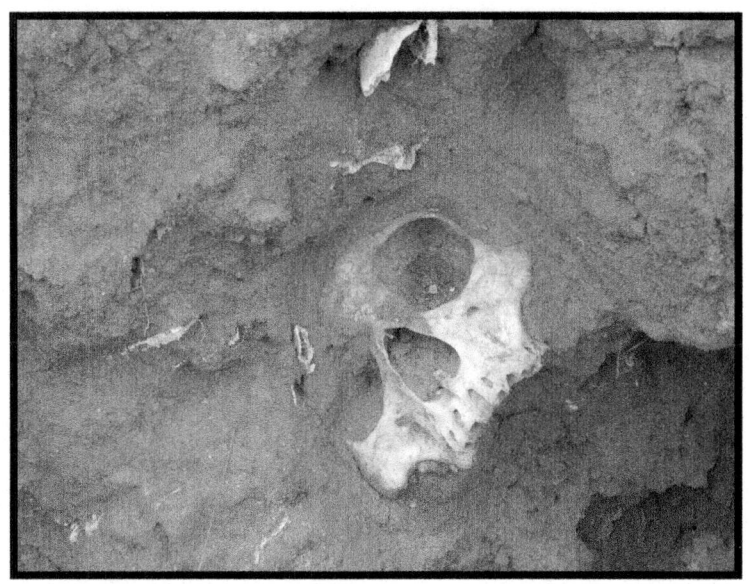

Skull found near Puma Punku on private property

The skull shown in the previous photo was discovered when a local man was constructing an out building several hundred yards to the west of Puma Punku, showing us that the ruins extend well beyond the fence that the government has built. Also found were hundreds of pottery shards of a refined nature and many shattered human bones.

The elongated skull was later stolen but there are 3 more on display in a small on site museum and I presume that this was one of or the royal cemetery of the Tiwanaku people. Over the course of time it is clear that other ancient artifacts will be dug up by farmers and unfortunately said artifacts will likely be sold to tourists as souvenirs. Such is the nature of a desolate location such as the little town of Tiwanaku where making a living is a daily struggle.

Red sandstone blocks with charred surfaces

Possibly melted surfaces on the sandstone

Other possible evidence of an ancient cataclysm at Puma Punku is seen above. Several smallish red

45

sandstone blocks show signs of high heat, much higher than a standard localized fire.

A last look at Puma Punku

We now move on to explore Tiwanaku which is in fact an extension of Puma Punku.

Model of Tiwanaku

As the site has suffered from looting and amateur excavations since shortly after Tiwanaku's fall, archeologists must attempt to interpret it with the understanding that materials have been jumbled and destroyed. This destruction continued during the Spanish conquest and colonial period, and during 19th century and the early 20th century. Other damage was committed by people quarrying stone for building and railroad construction, and target practice by military personnel.

No standing buildings have survived at the modern site. Only public, non-domestic foundations remain, with poorly reconstructed walls. The ashlar blocks used in many of these structures were mass-produced in similar styles so that they could possibly be used for multiple purposes. Throughout the period of the site, certain buildings changed purposes, causing a mix of artifacts found today.

Quadcopter view of the Kalasasaya

Detailed study of Tiwanaku began on a small scale in the mid-nineteenth century. In the 1860s, Ephraim George Squier visited the ruins and later published maps and sketches completed during his visit. German geologist Alphons Stübel spent nine days in Tiwanaku in 1876, creating a map of the site based on careful measurements. He also made sketches and created paper impressions of carvings and other architectural features. A book containing major photographic documentation was published in 1892 by engineer B. von Grumbkow. With commentary by archaeologist

Max Uhle, this was the first in-depth scientific account of the ruins.

Quadcopter view of the Akapana

In the 1960s, the Bolivian government initiated an effort to restore the site and reconstruct part of it. The walls of the Kalasasaya are almost all reconstructed. The original stones making up the Kalasasaya would have resembled a more "Stonehenge"-like style, spaced evenly apart and standing straight up. The reconstruction was not sufficiently based on research; for instance, a new wall was built around Kalasasaya. The reconstruction does not have as high quality of stonework as was present in Tiwanaku. As noted, the Gateway of the Sun, now in the Kalasasaya, was moved from its original location.

Tiwanaku is enclosed by fencing as is Puma Punku but the area of Tiwanaku is far larger. While little activity of the Tiwanaku people can be seen at Puma Punku, the Tiwanaku site seems to have been their epicenter.

Quadcopter view of the Kalasasaya and Sunken temple

Quadcopter view inside the Kalasasaya

As stated above, much of the "restoration" of Tiwanaku was based on theories that had no basis in actual facts, and as a result thousands of stones were moved without making accounts of their original positions.

Stones moved from other locations to build a wall

In the above photo you can see that stones were haphazardly put into place from various locations, mixing red sandstone and grey andesite in no particular order or pattern and in between massive andesite columns that show signs of extreme weathering.
As I showed at Puma Punku, the two types of stone were brought from their distant quarries because of the specific properties of the materials, not randomly thrown together. The academics who did this work showed total disregard for the brilliance of the original builders, and were eventually shut down by UNESCO

because of their lack of proper research and attention to detail.

Irene and the author: visit number 55?

As Tiwanaku is quite vast, and the alterations done to it in the name of "science" so extensive, we will begin in the fashion that we normally do when we visit this place, starting at the Akapana.

It is a tiered pyramidal structure originally having 7 levels and was made of tight fitting red sandstone blocks of medium size. Unfortunately the stones were generally of a size that a strong man could carry and thus a substantial number of them were removed to mainly build the massive church in the nearby small town of Tiwanaku, and others for the foundation of peoples' houses.

Stack of small blocks near the Akapana

From a distance the Akapana looks like a large mound of reddish clay mud and this is far more than what would have been the result of normal decay over the thousand years since the Tiwanaku people abandoned the area. It appears to me that the same mud wave cataclysm that largely buried Puma Punku was also responsible for turning a once pristine 7 tiered pyramidal structure into a natural looking mud hill, and the following photos of its excavation will shed further light on this idea.

A very bad job at "reconstruction' of the Akapana, likely in the 1960s was halted yet again by UNESCO, because instead of rebuilding in stone, the archaeologists used adobe mud bricks, once again making an enigmatic place even more confusing.

Author Antonio Portugal

Excavation at the Akapana removing the red clay

Photo showing depth of mud and red sandstone blocks

In the above 2 photos you can see that between 6 and 10 feet of the red clay mud covered much of the Akapana and in limited areas this was removed by archaeologists to expose the original red sandstone core. There is also extensive erosion of the stone surfaces at the bottom 6 feet of the original construction indicating that when Lake Titicaca was 100 feet higher than today, that the Akapana was an island. This, like Puma Punku would date the Akapana at being more than 12,000 years old.

Some 10,000 years later the Tiwanaku people found it buried in mud. They likely used it as a temple since it is the tallest structure in the area, and perhaps used some of the stones that had fallen from it for use in their own house construction. Amazingly, it is believed that at their peak the Tiwanaku people numbered more than 100,000, and since their homes were made of mud brick and thatch, only the original stone buildings still exist.

Irene pointing to a stone with high reading from a tesla meter

Some of the grey andesite at Tiwanaku shows the same magnetic anomalies as at Puma Punku and it was engineer Tony Marmont above who first used a tesla meter with us in the area.

A magnetometer is an instrument that measures magnetism, either the magnetization of a magnetic material like a ferromagnet, or the direction, strength, or relative change of a magnetic field at a particular location. A compass is a simple type of magnetometer, one that measures the direction of an ambient magnetic field.

The first magnetometer capable of measuring the absolute magnetic intensity was invented by Carl Friedrich Gauss in 1833 and notable developments in the 19th century included the Hall Effect, which is still widely used.

What is left of Tiwanaku buildings on the Akapana

Magnetometers are widely used for measuring the Earth's magnetic field and in geophysical surveys to detect magnetic anomalies of various types. They are also used in the military to detect submarines. Consequently, some countries, such as the United States, Canada and Australia, classify the more sensitive magnetometers as military technology, and control their distribution.

Remains of a gate on top of the Akapana

Detail of the broken gate

Andesite stone with magnetic anomalies

Massive andesite block now off limits

2 large andesite blocks with Chakana cross designs

Another example of archaeologists meddling with the site can be seen in the above photo. For many years these two large andesite blocks were like this, propped up on their sides. The one on the left was found facing down hiding the depressed design adopted by many cultures such as the Inca and called the Chakana. The other was found with the Chakana facing up and this can be surmised because the surface of the one on the left is still in good shape while the one on the right is highly weathered. Whether or not they were in fact found in this exact location is unknown but it is unlikely that they were not found buried underground due to the amount of weathering seen.

The 2 stones now propped up

Detail of the Chakana design

Taking photos of an excavation

We happened to be on location more than once when they were doing excavations somewhat near the Akapana. Technically photos were not allowed although they never told us why and so a few accidental pictures were taken. The most alarming thing about the excavations was that very large and well shaped slabs were excavated and rather than exposing more and more of them they immediately reburied them and in fact brought in more soil from other areas and increased the amount of dirt by 2 feet, covering up many of the stones of the site.

The idea that they were "protecting them" from the elements is quite ridiculous; they were in fact hiding the evidence.

Literally burying the truth

More of the evidence

Top of a foundation stone; amazingly level

Another level foundation stone

Extremely level

Strange semicircles; seem machined

Foundation and other andesite slabs

Tiwanaku culture recycled floor

Foundation stone with drill hole

Seemingly machined drill hole

Yousef Awyan inspecting multiple drill holes

Odd stone with compound curves

Detail photo of the compound curves

Flat andesite block affecting the compass

Megalithic stone used by Tiwanaku people as wash basins

Massive block with catastrophic break

Same stone after excavation added 2 feet of soil

Orange sandstone block now buried

72

Beautifully flat surfaces

More great flat surfaces

Ernie inspecting shattered fragments

Patricia and odd green stone

Anthony and another odd green stone

The green stones, of which I have seen about 15 examples at Tiwanaku and Puma Punku are anomalies and their source quarry has not yet been figured out. There are many ancient mines in the altiplano area and copper has been used as a trade item to locations as far away as Cusco, the coast of Peru and even Ecuador.

Fortunately samples were sent to a laboratory in the United States and were analyzed for content; the results showed that 36% was copper, much higher than required in order to process in a smelter. One theory is that Puma Punku and Tiwanaku were originally constructed as metallic ore processing facilities, and since bronze clamps have been found in the area and were in fact poured into place leaves this as a possibility.

Close up of the interesting green stone

View of Sunken temple and Kalasasaya

Sunken temple

Why the Sunken temple was built below the surface while all others are above ground is curious, and could relate to the smelting facility theory. There is a tunnel and shaft system that goes from the top of the Akapana and leads straight to the center of the Sunken temple. The possible reasoning behind this could be that the ore was ground up and fed with lots of water through the shaft and tunnel system and that the Sunken temple acted as a settling pond.

The ore, being heavier than water would settle to the bottom, and after a period of time an elaborate drainage system, that still exists in the Sunken temple would be opened up to release the water. Then the ore would be collected and processed in the smelter.

Author David Hatcher Childress in the Sunken temple

The author with bearded Wiracocha statue

Some of the heads in the wall

Details of the heads, some wearing turbans

Original entrance into the Kalasasaya

Detail of the entrance with eroded steps

"Reconstructed wall" at the north end of the Kalasasaya

Original drainage pipe recycled into the wall

Vertical megalithic columns showing extreme weathering

Tiwanaku culture wall reconstruction

Andesite stone with Tiwanaku culture etching

Detail of the Tiwanaku carving

Sections of water channels on display

Colonial period unfinished grinding wheel

More drainage channels and grinding wheel

Drainage channel with interesting even grooves

Antonio and Renee at the Sun Gate

One ruin still standing in Tiahuanaco is the Gate of the Sun. The Gate of the Sun is approximately 3 meters tall and carved on a single block of stone, weighing at least 10 tons. When rediscovered by European explorers in the mid 19th century, the megalith was lying horizontally and had a large crack going through it. It currently stands in the same location where It was found, although it is believed that this is not its original location, which remains uncertain.

The figures that decorate the stone are believed to have astronomical connotations and resemble human-like beings with wings and curled-up tails, and appear to be wearing rectangular 'helmets', although interpretations differ. The ' Sun-God' is in the center and is sculpted with rays emitting from his face in all directions. He also appears to be holding a staff in each hand. The 'Sun-God' figure is also called the 'Weeping God' because things similar to tears are carved on its face.

Back side of the Sun Gate

Some people believe that this 'gate' was used as a calendar, causing some to call it 'the Calendar Gate'. Indeed, it appears to reflect a solar year, however, it cannot be made to fit into the solar year as we divide it at present. The calendar has 290 days, divided into twelve months of 24 days each. Other radical theories suggest it was a portal to another dimension, perhaps to the 'land of the gods'.

Of particular note is that the back of the Sun Gate is far more heavily weathered than the front, so it is very likely that the Tiwanaku people found it face down, and broken into 2 pieces. They then re-erected it and etched the surface carvings into the front.

The Moon Gate

The so called Moon Gate is located several hundred meters from the Sun Gate but is also within the main fence of Tiwanaku. It was made from one piece of andesite and fortunately is still intact, weighing about 6 tons.
It is likely that the ancient cataclysm of about 12,000 years ago caused the Sun Gate to fall down and be snapped in 2; the fact that the Moon Gate is still intact is quite amazing being that it is thinner and more delicate than the Sun Gate.

Another precise surface

And another

Amazing precise angle

Insert area showing dovetail angle

Huge slab at that archaeologists recently partially reburied

Wiracocha statue made from Puma Punku andesite

92

Another channel section with parallel groove marks

Subterranean chamber seemingly water tight

Very rare book with classic early photos

Original Kalasasaya wall

a. Sun Door in front view (year 1904).
Puerta del Sol, vista de frente (año 1904).

The Sun Gate

The Sun Gate reconstructed

Tiwanaku people resurrecting the Sun Gate

The Sun Gate as found by the Spanish

Entrance to the Kalasasaya

Early Tiwanaku excavations

Figure 37. Excavation of the French Mission on the site where the subterranean dwellings were found.
Excavación de la misión francesa en el sitio donde halláronse las habitaciones subterráneas.

Earliest excavations

Figure 38. Subterranean dwellings found by the French Mission near the balcony wall of the Sun Temple (Cf. Pl. 3, location V of the map of Tihuanacu in Vol. I).
Habitaciones subterráneas halladas por la misión francesa cerca de la pared balconera del templo del Sol (Véase Plancha 3, sitio V del plano de Tihuanacu en el I Tomo).

Excavations now reburied

Figure 46. Main block of Kantataita, pattern or model of a building of Tihuanacu.
Bloque principal de Kantataita, modelo o maqueta de un edificio Tihuanacu.

Massive slab at Tiwanaku

Figure 46a. External westerly part of the Kantataita group.
Parte externa hacia el Oeste del grupo Kantataita.

South of the Akapana

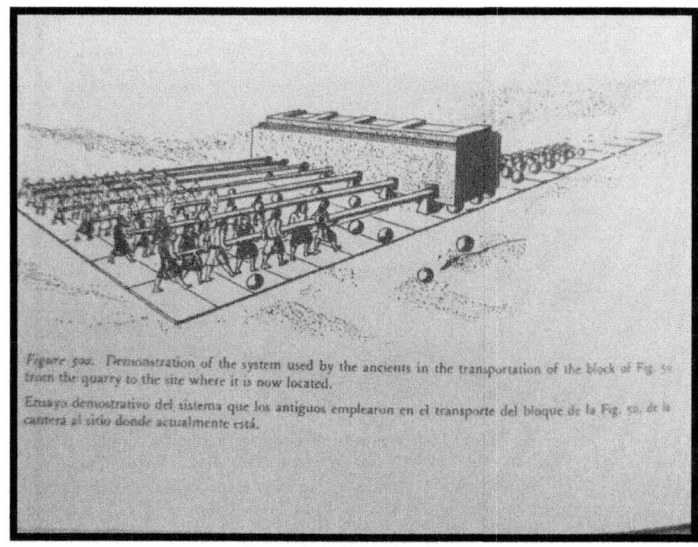

Figure 50a. Demonstration of the system used by the ancients in the transportation of the block of Fig. 50 from the quarry to the site where it is now located.

Ensayo demostrativo del sistema que los antiguos emplearon en el transporte del bloque de la Fig. 50, de la cantera al sitio donde actualmente está.

Completely ridiculous

Puma Punku with 4 H blocks

More of Puma Punku

ure 53. Parts of the west wall of the Moon Temple composed of blocks cut from extremely hard andesite on which carved the typical niches.

rtes de la pared Oeste del templo de la Luna compuestas de bloques tallados en durísima andesita, en las cuales están ladas las típicas hornacinas o nichos.

H blocks

More early photos

In situ

Found half buried in the ground

Village house early 20th century

House made from Puma Punku

The village cemetery

Printed in Great Britain
by Amazon